Taught Us
to Pray

# "By Your Name"

ISBN 978-1-0877-5210-5
Item 005834387
Dewey Decimal Classification Number: 242
Subject Heading: DEVOTIONAL LITERATURE / BIBLE STUDY AND TEACHING / GOD

Printed in the United States of America

Student Ministry Publishing
Lifeway Resources
One Lifeway Plaza
Nashville, Tennessee 37234

We believe that the Bible has God for its author; salvation for its end; and truth, without any mixture of error, for its matter and that all Scripture is totally true and trustworthy. To review Lifeway's doctrinal guideline, please visit www.lifeway.com/doctrinalguideline.

# publishing team

*Director, Student Ministry*
Ben Trueblood

*Manager, Student Ministry Publishing*
John Paul Basham

*Editorial Team Leader*
Karen Daniel

*Writer*
Alyssa Lewis

*Content Editor*
Stephanie Cross

*Production Editor*
Brooke Hill

*Graphic Designer*
Shiloh Stufflebeam

# Table of Contents

# Intro

There is no "right" way to pray. There is no script that will make more of your prayers reach God. There is no elegant language that will make Him listen to you more. And there is certainly no magical combination of words that will grant you whatever you ask. Prayer is just you bringing your most authentic self before a Father who just wants you to know Him.

If it's that simple, you may ask, why is it so hard to pray? Prayer is simple communication, but it's also an important spiritual discipline—and discipline requires sacrifice. Prayer requires you to sacrifice your time, your pride, and your own will for God's will. That sacrifice can seem like a lot, and you may not know where to start—but don't worry! There is good news: during His time on earth, Jesus took all the guesswork out of prayer by doing every single thing He asks you to do. He has given you the ultimate example through His Word of how to pray.

In this devotional, you will learn when Jesus prayed, how He prayed, and what He prayed for. The intention of exploring these things is not so that you adopt a rigid set of rules to follow. Jesus understands that every one of His people is different and everyone is not meant to pray the same way. He wants to teach you to pray so you can understand the power it holds. If just the single mention of His name can work a miracle (see Acts 3:6), imagine how much more can He do in and through you when you daily call upon His name in prayer.

The greatest thing you can gain from the next thirty days would be a deeper understanding of the God who loves you and a closer relationship with Him through a more committed and genuine prayer life.

# Getting Started

This devotional contains thirty days of content, broken down into sections. Each day is divided into three elements—discover, delight, and display—to help you grow in your faith.

## discover |

This section helps you examine the passage in light of who God is and determine what it says about your identity in relationship to Him. Included here is the daily Scripture reading and key verses, along with illustrations and commentary to guide you as you learn more about God's Word.

## delight |

In this section, you'll be challenged by questions and activities that help you see how God is alive and active in every detail of His Word and your life.

## display |

Here's where you take action. Display calls you to apply what you've learned each day through activities and challenges.

> **Each day also includes a prayer activity at the conclusion of the devotion.**

Throughout the devotional, you'll also find extra articles and activities to help you connect with the topic personally, such as Scripture memory verses, additional resources, and quotes from leading Christian voices.

# When Jesus Prayed

This section outlines when Jesus prayed, which, as you'll see, was pretty much all the time. He prayed about big decisions, when He was in pain, just to give thanks, and for many other reasons. He embodied what it meant to "pray without ceasing" so that you can learn to do the same.

# It's Just Talking

## discover |

### LUKE 3:21-22.

*When all the people were baptized, Jesus also was baptized. As he was praying, heaven opened, and the Holy Spirit descended on him in a physical appearance like a dove. And a voice came from heaven: "You are my beloved Son; with you I am well-pleased."*

We meet Jesus at the point in His story when He got baptized in the Jordan River by John the Baptist (appropriate name, right?). Jesus's baptism was an act of obedience to the Father. He didn't need to be baptized as a symbol of repentance like you and I do; He was perfect, unlike us.

His baptism was an act of humility. He was fully God, but He was identifying with us as fully human to give us an example of how to live. Jesus made Himself a living example of so many other things too—especially prayer.

As Jesus prayed after He was baptized, God the Father spoke to Him from heaven. When He spoke, He specifically identified His relationship with Jesus ("my beloved Son") and gave Him His blessing ("with you I am well-pleased"). Those two things are important because, though Jesus has had a relationship with the Father since the beginning, when He came to earth, He communicated to God through prayer, just like we do. Jesus was in constant communication with God in good times and in really difficult times (see Matt. 15:36; John 17).

How can you truly, deeply love someone without first getting to know them? And how do you get to know them? By talking to them! That's all prayer is—talking to God. The more you talk to Him, the more you will know Him. The more you know Him, the more you will love Him.

# delight |

What would your relationship with your best friend look like if you didn't talk to each other for days, weeks, or months at a time?

Do you think God would identify you as His "beloved" daughter? Why or why not? (Hint: see John 1:12.)

# display |

Take a moment to really think about prayer. The God who created the entire universe and every piece of you wants to be in relationship with you. He has given you 24/7 access to Him to talk about anything and everything. See the prayer section below and take the next five minutes to intentionally pray through the guide, focusing your heart on the reality that Jesus wants to hear from you.

**Start by thanking Jesus for the gift of prayer. Thank Him for the fact that He could have created you and stopped there, but He wants a relationship with you. Ask Him to forgive you when you don't make time to talk to Him. He knows you better than anyone else, so share your life with Him. Talk to Him about how you want to know Him more too.**

# More Than Just Sleep

## discover |

READ LUKE 5:15-16.

*But the news about him spread even more, and large crowds would
come together to hear him and to be healed of their sicknesses. Yet
he often withdrew to deserted places and prayed.*

In the beginning of Luke 5, Jesus had just performed two of His
most famous miracles: filling the disciples' boats with fish (vv. 1-11)
and healing the leper (vv. 12-14). Even in the chapters before, Jesus
had been performing miracles left and right. He drew large crowds,
garnered a following, and moved many hearts from unbelief to belief.
Yet He often withdrew to deserted places and prayed. It is obvious from
the thriving state of His ministry that Jesus was in lockstep with the
Father, living out a deep relationship with Him—but Jesus still didn't
forsake time with Him.

This verse isn't saying Jesus was just an introvert who needed to
recharge His social batteries. That interpretation removes the
intentionality behind the action that the Lord wants you to understand.
Jesus took the opportunity to spend uninterrupted time with God in
prayer because He understood something that He also wants you to
know: true rest is more than just sleep.

You can spend your time doing good things for the Lord, but you can't
rely on only doing good things to deepen your relationship with Him.
If Jesus took time from performing actual miracles to talk to God, how
much more do you need to make time with Him a priority? Your time
alone with Him is what grows your love for Him, and your love for Him
is what fuels your service to Him.

# delight |

**What in your life do you use as a substitute for true rest?**

**What is the "crowd" you need to step away from in order to spend time with the Lord?**

# display |

Just like we talked about yesterday, Jesus wants to hear from you! Taking time to talk to Him not only gives rest to your body but also to your mind and your emotions. When you've rested with Him, your capacity to do things for Him expands.

Do your best to take ten minutes each day for the rest of the week to talk with God. Pay attention to how rested you feel after this and journal your thoughts on how that compares to other ways you try to rest.

Name some girls you know who also need rest. Spend some time praying for them and, if they know the Lord, encouraging them to find rest in prayer too!

**Lord, I confess that I've chosen things over You that I thought would bring me rest. Sometimes it's easier to stay with the crowd than to choose You. Remind me that there has never been a moment when I've regretted stepping away and stepping toward You instead. Help me find my rest in You.**

# While It Was Still Dark

## discover |

READ MARK 1:35-38.

*Very early in the morning, while it was still dark, he got up, went out, and made his way to a deserted place; and there he was praying.*
*—Mark 1:35*

Waking up in the morning is so hard, right? When my alarm goes off, my mind instantly lists all of the corners I can cut in my morning beauty routine just to get an extra ten minutes of sleep. But Jesus chose to begin His day with the Father—early—even after teaching all day and healing late into the night before. He had every reason to sleep in. He could have told God, "Look at all of the miracles I'm doing for You!" or "Look how many people have chosen to follow You because of my teaching! I'm just going to take an extra ten before we load up the donkeys and head to the next town." Instead, Jesus chose to start His day alone with His Father to prepare for the day ahead. He understood where He got His strength; He knew He couldn't make it through everything life would throw at Him—like actual demons and Satan himself (see Matt. 4:1-11; Mark 1:21-28)—without spending time with God first.

There's another part of this Scripture that's very important to notice. Jesus "made his way to a deserted place" to pray. He got alone and rid Himself of all distractions so He could spend uninterrupted time with the Father. I know that even though Jesus was praying while it was still dark, He left that alone time with God more rested than before, ready to take on the day and meet every challenge with faith instead of fear.

# delight |

**Why did Jesus choose to spend time with God while it was still dark?**

**How would your day change if you started it by talking to Jesus?**

# display |

It must be said: you can still spend time with God even if you're not a morning person. There is no shame in meeting with Jesus at night! There can be a certain relief that comes with casting all of the cares that you've accumulated throughout the day on Him. Whatever time of day you meet with Him, He just asks that you do it alone and free of distractions (yes, that includes your phone). Find a place today—your closet, your car, your bed at night, your backyard—to be alone with God. Let all of the pressure and busyness of life move you toward God, not away from Him. In the space below, describe or sketch where you will meet with God today.

Lord, it is so easy to value more time in bed over more time with You. Help me make You the number one priority in my life around which I build my day. Thank You for Your grace that allows me to start fresh with You every morning. I trust that You will speak to me as I sacrifice more time asleep for more time spent with You.

# Big Decision, Bigger God

## discover |

READ LUKE 6:12-16.

*During those days he went out to the mountain to pray and spent all
night in prayer to God. When daylight came, he summoned his disciples,
and he chose twelve of them, whom he also named apostles.*
—Luke 6:12–13

I have stayed up all night multiple times in my life—studying, at
sleepovers, or on road trips. However, not once have I ever stayed
awake until sunrise because I was praying. That's exactly what Jesus did
in the verses you just read. He went out to the mountain to talk to God
about who to choose as His twelve disciples. As we've talked about
before, Jesus had many followers; there was always a crowd of people
to hear Him teach or watch Him perform a miracle. Jesus had to choose
who to invite into His close circle, and that was not a decision He took
lightly. His disciples would be the ones to carry on the work He started,
taking the message of good news throughout the earth. Jesus knew He
needed to talk to the Father about such a big decision.

It's important for you to pray about big decisions too! Prayer not only
allows you to talk to the Lord, but it also allows the Lord to talk to you.
Jeremiah 29:11 makes clear that God wants what's best for you. If you
read just a verse further, you'll see He wants to talk to you about your
decisions. From choosing friendships to choosing what you want to do
with your life, Jesus cares. When you trust that God's plan for you is
good, you can talk to Him about your biggest, scariest decisions and
trust that He will guide you to what's best.

# delight |

**Read Jeremiah 29:11-13. What does that Scripture say about what happens when you pray about the decisions in your life?**

**How does knowing God has an answer for your biggest decisions change the way you pray?**

# display |

When you have a difficult decision to make, talking to your parents or friends seems like a great option. And it is! But even they don't know you like God knows you. During your time alone with the Lord today, spend five minutes praying about a decision you have to make, and spend another five minutes in silence, taking time to listen for an answer. You may be surprised by how clearly you hear Him speak. Even if you don't feel like you're hearing from Him, continue praying for an answer each day, trusting that He wants to guide you.

While no one else knows you like God does, it can also be a great idea to ask some close girl friends and mentors to pray for you as you make a big decision. You don't have to tell them what it is; just ask them to pray. Name a few girls and women you could ask to pray for you as you're making those decisions.

Thank You, Lord, for caring so deeply about every part of my life. Help me trust that You know me best, and that means You know what's best for my life. This decision I have to make has been weighing on me, and I want to let You guide me. I give You control of the outcome, and I will follow where You lead me.

*"By Your Name"*

# 5+2=1, or 12?

## discover |

READ LUKE 9:10-17.

*Then he took the five loaves and the two fish, and looking up to heaven, he blessed and broke them. He kept giving them to the disciples to set before the crowd. Everyone ate and was filled. They picked up twelve baskets of leftover pieces.*
—*Luke 9:16-17*

Five loaves and two fish. Even if you haven't known of Jesus for very long, there is a very good chance you know this story. Earlier in the story, Jesus sent the twelve disciples out to preach the gospel and perform miracles from village to village (see Luke 9:1-6). When they returned, Jesus and the twelve withdrew from the crowds so Jesus could hear all about what they had done. However, the crowds found out where they had gone and met them there. Because they were in a "deserted place" (v. 12), the people in the crowd had no place to stay and nothing to eat. Jesus could have chosen to send the people away as the disciples requested, but He chose to meet their needs instead. Before passing out the food, He prayed and blessed it, or thanked God for providing it. God honored that prayer and the fact that Jesus chose to provide for the crowd by multiplying the little that He had.

You may be a high-capacity girl when it comes to serving the Lord, but without prayer, you are sure to fall short. Strength to serve the Lord can only come from the Lord! Asking Him to bless the work of your hands is admitting that you can't do anything on your own and giving Him all the glory for the outcome. He always wants to hear from you, and He is always ready to help you bless others in His name.

# delight |

Imagine being in the crowd that day. What would you have thought about Jesus after seeing Him perform that miracle?

How does it motivate you to pray for Jesus to bless the work of your hands knowing that He's the same One who multiplied the small amount of fish and bread?

*"By Your Name"*

# display |

One of the ways people know you love Jesus is by your actions. However, it can be very easy to grow weary of doing good when you do it in your own strength. That's why Jesus asks you to come to Him.

Pray through the guided prayer below and ask for help as you seek to glorify God through your work.

Then, prayerfully list some actions you can take to show the girls around you your love for Jesus this week.

Lord, thank You for the opportunity to bring glory to Your name by serving others. I want to be an example of Your love as much as possible! Please multiply my efforts and energy just like You multiplied the bread and fish as I look for new chances to serve every day.

# Whose Are You?

## discover |

### READ LUKE 9:18-20.

*While he was praying in private and his disciples were with him, he asked them, "Who do the crowds say that I am?" They answered, "John the Baptist; others, Elijah; still others, that one of the ancient prophets has come back." "But you," he asked them, "who do you say that I am?" Peter answered, "God's Messiah."*

My sister is one of my closest friends. I talk to her constantly, and I see her every chance I get. All of my friends know about her because I talk about her all the time, and they want to meet her because they can tell how much I love her. I'm sure you talk about the people you love too. It would be kind of weird if you didn't.

Jesus set an example of prayer for the disciples that made it clear He was sent from and connected to God. Rising early in the morning and spending time alone in prayer is what fueled Jesus as He taught the gospel and performed miracles. Peter knew Jesus was the Messiah, sent from God, because God revealed it to him (see Matt. 16:17).

In the same way, how you pray shows who you're connected to. Spending time with the Lord changes you in such a way that who you are in public is a direct reflection of who you spend time with in private. Even more than your family, classmates, or your best friend, let the greatest influence in your life be Jesus.

# delight |

**Do you think people can tell if you spend time with the Lord by the way you act? Why or why not?**

**When you spend a lot of time with someone, you begin to adopt some of their mannerisms, habits, and words. What things do you do as a result of spending time with the Lord?**

# display |

In 1 Corinthians 11:1, Paul told the church in Corinth "Imitate me, as I also imitate Christ." In other words, "I am following the Lord so intimately that you should watch me closely and do everything that I do."

Think about your life right now and ask yourself if you can say the same thing. If you can, praise God! Pray and thank Him for the way He is working in your life. If not, pray and ask God what in your life needs to change for there to be no question in the minds of others that you belong to Him.

Now, think about the girls around you and the women in your life. Who lives like Paul and Jesus, worthy of imitation? Take a minute to think of godly traits they have that you'd like to imitate and jot those down. Then, consider sending a text or even writing a note to tell them what their influence has meant to you.

Lord, I confess that often, I can see more ways I'm not like You than the ways I am. With a humble heart, I ask You to make me more like You. I want to be someone who draws people to You when I say I'm a Christian, not someone who pushes them further away. I trust that You will change me the more time I spend with You.

MEMORY VERSE

*John 11:41-42*

SO THEY REMOVED THE STONE. THEN
JESUS RAISED HIS EYES AND SAID,
"FATHER, I THANK YOU THAT YOU
HEARD ME. I KNOW THAT YOU ALWAYS
HEAR ME, BUT BECAUSE OF THE
CROWD STANDING HERE I SAID THIS,
SO THAT THEY MAY BELIEVE YOU
SENT ME."

# Nothing Is Impossible

## discover |

READ LUKE 9:28-36.

*About eight days after this conversation, he took along Peter, John, and James
and went up on the mountain to pray. As he was praying, the appearance of
his face changed, and his clothes became dazzling white. Suddenly, two men
were talking with him — Moses and Elijah. They appeared in glory and were
speaking of his departure, which he was about to accomplish in Jerusalem.*
*—Luke 9:28-31*

This is the story of what is commonly referred to as the transfiguration.
Jesus had just finished telling His disciples that He was going to die on
the cross and that they should pick up their own crosses and follow Him
(see Luke 9:21-22). Jesus was talking about spiritually dying to themselves
and their desires daily just as He was going to physically die on the cross.
It could have sounded very discouraging to the disciples to hear that the
leader they had been following and trusted to be the Messiah was going to
die. Little did they know, this experience would bring a moment of renewed
faith. As He was praying, Jesus's face and clothes changed, giving those with
Him a glimpse of His glory, proving that He was who He said He was and
that He was worth following.

Prayer allows Jesus to give you a glimpse of His glory. It may not be a
physical glimpse like in Scripture, but He can do life-changing things
that show His power. He can heal a sick body. He can restore a broken
relationship you thought was past the point of reconciliation. He can help
you make it through each day as you struggle with depression. God is still
a God of wonders. The same One who refused to let death have the final
word has not run out of miracles to do in your life. All you have to do is pray.

# delight |

**Is it difficult for you to believe God still performs miracles? Why or why not?**

**How does understanding that God can do life-changing things through prayer change the way you pray?**

*"By Your Name"*

# display |

Prayer isn't something you're commanded to do as just another box to check on a list of what it means to be a "good Christian." The Lord longs to do big, life-changing things for you and through you. Think of one thing you want the Lord to do in your life or the life of a girl you know that seems impossible. Follow the prayer outline below and ask the Lord to show you a glimpse of His glory in this situation.

Lord, my mind is human and finite, and I confess that it's hard for me to understand the extent of what You can do. This thing feels really big and impossible to me, but I know You have the power to do anything. As I pray each day, help me trust that You are who You say You are and pray with absolute confidence that You will change my life.

# Practicing Prayer

## discover |

### READ LUKE 11:1.

*He was praying in a certain place, and when he finished, one of his disciples said to him, "Lord, teach us to pray, just as John also taught his disciples."*

Have you ever seen someone so disciplined at something that you wonder how they do it? I have a friend who wakes up early to run before starting her day. Another friend of mine studies Greek in his spare time just because he wants to learn.

When I see the time and effort they put into their individual pursuits, I don't question how to do them—I know how to study, I just don't. I know how to run, I just don't. I know how to wake up early, and I definitely don't.

The disciples didn't ask Jesus how to pray; they asked Him to teach them to pray, to teach them the spiritual discipline of prayer. Jesus wants you to understand that it doesn't matter how you pray. It could be out loud or in silence, in your room or in your car, eyes closed or eyes open—He just wants you to pray. The way you pray can reflect Jesus to other people in the same way Jesus's prayer reflected His relationship with God to the disciples. To be clear, you don't pray just to inspire others; prayer is intimate communication between you and the Father. But when you pray, things change. The way you treat your family, the way you talk to (and about) others, and the things you sacrifice to spend time with God will be direct reflections of your time in prayer.

# delight |

**Whose relationship with the Lord influences you to spend more time with Him? What can you do that they model?**

**Do you think your relationship with the Lord inspires others? How can you grow in your relationship with Him to be a greater inspiration to others?**

# display |

Your relationship with the Lord is personal, yes, but it doesn't have to be secret. Let your prayer life be like that of Jesus: captivating. You may be thinking, "I don't spend time with God on a mountainside. No one is around to see me pray." Invite other girls into your prayer life by asking how you can pray for them—and then diligently pray for them. Watch as your relationships with those girls deepen alongside your relationship with the Lord. If you don't already, begin a note on your phone or in a small notepad you carry around with you called "Prayer List." When the people in your life mention prayer requests, put them on this list and pray over them regularly.

Jesus, teach me to pray. I confess that on the days I "just don't feel like it," what I really mean is that I don't want to sacrifice my time or energy to spend time with You. Help me choose You every day over everything else. Grow me in the discipline of prayer until it becomes second nature.

# Are You There, God?

## discover |

### READ JOHN 11:38-44.

*So they removed the stone. Then Jesus raised his eyes and said, "Father, I thank you that you heard me. I know that you always hear me, but because of the crowd standing here I said this, so that they may believe you sent me."*
*—John 11:41–42*

Lazarus returning from the dead is a pivotal moment in the earthly ministry of Jesus. Not only was it perhaps the most "difficult" miracle Jesus performed, but it also set in motion the Jewish leaders' plan to arrest (and later crucify) Him for calling Himself the Messiah. Even so, my favorite thing about this story is how well it showcases the humanity of Jesus.

Lazarus was not an arbitrary follower of Jesus or just another face in the crowd. The passage makes it clear that Lazarus and his family were close friends of Jesus (see John 11:5), and He was deeply grieved by the death of His dear friend. It is evident in the prayer Jesus prayed before raising Lazarus from the dead that He had been in prayer in the days before. He didn't cry out to God on His friend's behalf for the first time in front of the tomb; He thanked God for already hearing Him.

This is so important in your relationship with Jesus because you can pray with complete confidence, knowing He hears you and He understands. He is not an unbothered, far-off entity watching you figure out life on your own; Jesus is with you always. He has felt everything you feel, and He wants you to come talk to Him.

# delight |

What is something in your life that feels too big to pray for?

What is an obstacle to God hearing your prayers? (Hint: Read Psalm 66:17-20.)

What do you think God could do in your life without the obstacle of unconfessed sin?

# display |

When Jesus heard the news of Lazarus's death, He waited two days before going to him—not because He was unmoved by his death, but because He wanted to perform the miracle in God's timing. Knowing that the Lord hears you when you pray should motivate you to pray with boldness. He may not answer right away, but His delay is not a denial.

Choose one thing to pray about this week that feels too big to pray for and pray about it with boldness, knowing He hears you.

Write out the name of a girl you know who might be asking, "Are you there, God?" Take some time to encourage her that God hears her and pray bold prayers with her.

I praise You, Lord, for being the same God I read about in the Bible. If You heard the prayers of Your people then, I know You hear mine now. Thank You for coming to earth as a man because I know You understand everything I could possibly experience. I know You can do anything. Help me pray big prayers and trust in the timing of Your answer.

# *Forgiven*

## discover |

READ LUKE 23:34.

*Then Jesus said, "Father, forgive them, because they do not know what they are doing." And they divided his clothes and cast lots.*

In the hours leading up to Jesus's crucifixion, He endured a devastating series of torments. He was betrayed by Judas, one of the closest people to Him. He was tried before the government as a criminal and took the place of a murderer on the cross. He was beaten, stripped of His clothing, and mocked. (A more detailed account can be found in Matthew 27:1-49.) Even after all of that, He chose to endure the cross—the worst form of public torture, designed to kill slowly with the maximum amount of pain one could bear while staying conscious. And Jesus took upon Himself the guilt and sin of the world, experiencing the full wrath of God.

With all of that in mind, revisit the Scripture for the day: "Then Jesus said, 'Father, forgive them.'" After suffering the worst physical, emotional, and spiritual pain, Jesus still chose to pray forgiveness and mercy toward His tormentors. He was on the cross asking God to forgive the very people who put Him there.

That kind of radical prayer does not have to be exclusive to Jesus. There will be hurt in your life that will feel too difficult to pray about— girls you think you'll never be able to forgive. Whether or not they "do not know what they are doing," they can still be forgiven—by God and by you. It may take a little longer for you to forgive them, and that's okay. You can ask God to help you. He will.

# delight |

**Why is it hard to forgive?**

**How does following God's example of forgiveness help you forgive?**

# display |

It would be simple to dismiss Jesus's prayer for His enemies, thinking He was able to forgive them because of His divinity. It's true that Jesus already knew all that was going to happen to Him, but being fully God and fully man, He was still physically wounded and emotionally hurt. Whether you have hurt from an enemy or from a friend, Jesus covered it on the cross. Following His example, pray today for a girl who has hurt you. Ask the Lord to forgive her, and ask Him to help you forgive her. Write the word "forgiven" below and just dwell on it. Dwell on the reality that you have been forgiven and that God can help you forgive others.

Thank You, Lord, for giving Yourself as the sacrifice for sin. You made a way for forgiveness—for me and for those who hurt me. I confess that it is sometimes hard to forgive; it's hard to get over hurt. I surrender my hurt and anger to You. Help me to forgive by reminding me of how greatly I've been forgiven.

# How Jesus Taught Us To Pray

The way Jesus taught us to pray is less about rules and structure and more about having a right view of God and right motivation of the heart. In this section, you will learn that understanding the power and holiness of God changes the way you pray.

# Audience of One

## discover |

*But when you pray, go into your private room, shut your door, and pray to your*
*Father who is in secret. And your Father who sees in secret will reward you.*
*—Matthew 6:6*

Jews living in the time of Jesus had a few opportunities to pray in public places. At the right time of day, they could go to the synagogue, or Jewish temple, or on the street and pray out loud. Unfortunately, those spots were often chosen by hypocrites trying to be seen praying in public. They prayed so others could marvel at their masterful language and elevated spirituality. But should either of those things be the motivation behind prayer? Absolutely not. That's why Jesus instructed the disciples to do as He often did: pray in seclusion.

When you are by yourself, there is no one to impress. I've performed many songs and choreographed countless dance routines for the most captivated audience: me, myself, and I. My mirror doesn't care if I look good, and my hairbrush doesn't care if I sound good; everything I do is simply for personal amusement. When you pray alone, you have an audience of one: Jesus. He doesn't care if you use fancy words. He doesn't care what you look like. He doesn't judge your prayer in any way. The Lord's instruction to pray in privacy is so that you can come to Him as your most genuine, humble self. There is no pressure to impress; He loves you as you are. Save the performance for your hairbrush and mirror.

*Lifeway Girls | Devotions*     42

# delight |

**What places have been your synagogues and street corners (places where you've prayed primarily for peoples' attention)?**

**How does praying in private help you focus on just talking to Jesus from your heart?**

*"By Your Name"*

# display |

This passage of Scripture isn't a free pass to never pray in public again. What the Lord is trying to say is that the motivation of your heart is what matters the most whenever and wherever you pray. When you pray in public, is your motivation to teach or impress others? When you pray in private, is your motivation to just check a box and be done for the day? Write out the words of Psalm 139:23-24. Be as creative as you like. Use this Scripture to guide you as you examine your heart with the Lord today.

Examine my heart, God, and reveal to me anything that's not of You. I'm sorry for the times when I've prayed just to affect other people and not because I just wanted to talk to You. Remind me that all I have to offer You is me—and that's enough for You.

# Anytime, Anywhere

## discover |

READ MATTHEW 6:9A.

*"Therefore, you should pray like this: Our Father in heaven . . ."*

Have you ever called an adult Mr. or Mrs., just for them to tell you to call them by their first name? It feels like an honor but also kind of weird and maybe even a bit disrespectful.

There is no evidence in the Bible of anyone calling God "Father" before Jesus. Jews at the time thought it to be too intimate, not fully capturing the reverence they were supposed to have for God. So I'm sure you can imagine the glances the disciples exchanged when Jesus told them they could pray by saying "Our Father." They probably felt honored that they could talk to God in such a personal way, but it probably also felt unnatural and irreverent to address Him like that.

Addressing Him as "Our Father in heaven" covers all of that. "Our Father" denotes your closeness in relationship. "In heaven" is indicative of His divinity and holiness. And how incredible is it that the One who is closer to you than anyone is also the Savior of the world?

The Lord's Prayer is a template, not a script. Jesus said, "pray *like* this." You don't have to pray the exact words of the Lord's Prayer each time you pray. All He's asking is that you come to Him in reverence of His holiness and in complete security in your identity as His daughter. You can talk to Him anytime, anywhere.

# delight |

Jot down the name of a girl in your life you feel like you can always talk to.


Read Psalm 121:4. How is the access you have to God different from the access you have to people?


How does understanding that you have unlimited, 24/7 access to God help you live out 1 Thessalonians 5:17 and "pray constantly"?

# display |

Each person's relationship with their earthly father is different. Maybe you and your dad are incredibly close. Maybe you just orbit around each other and try not to push each other's buttons. Maybe you don't even speak to one another. Whatever your relationship may be, your Father in heaven knows every detail of your life and cares about it all. Try praying without ceasing today. Invite Him into even the smallest moments—a disagreement with a friend, a frustration with a teacher, a sibling getting on your nerves—and talk to Him about them!

Lord, thank You for being with me at all times. Remind me that I can talk to You whenever I need to, even in the moments that feel too small. Help me to come to You first before anyone else. You know me best, and I trust that You will lead me in the way that's best for me.

# For the Sake of Christ

## discover |

READ MATTHEW 6:9B.

*". . .your name be honored as holy."*

I have a very special favorite mug. I got it all the way in Greece, and it has a lovely rendering of the city of Athens on it. I rarely let anyone use this mug; it stays on a special shelf, and I only wash it by hand. I honor it in those ways because it's so precious to me, and I don't have any other mug like it.

I'm sure you also treat the things that are precious to you with respect—nice shoes, costly electronics, or fine jewelry. Moreover, I'm sure you treat the people who are precious to you with respect. Your relationship with Jesus should be the most sacred to you, and He asks that you treat it as such. To honor the Lord's name as holy when you pray means that you approach Him with reverence, acknowledging His power and perfection.

The Bible regards the name of Jesus in the highest possible terms. Acts 4:12 says, "There is salvation in no one else, for there is no other name under heaven given to people by which we must be saved." Another word for vain is *emptiness*. Using the Lord's name in vain as merely an exclamation strips from it all reverence that it's due. His name heals the sick and raises the dead; it is far too powerful to be used as an empty filler where so many other words would suffice. I think you can expand your vocabulary for the actual sake of Christ.

# delight |

In your everyday vocabulary, do you use Lord's name in vain? If so how can you change that? If not, how can you encourage others not to misuse the name of the Lord?

How do you know there is power in the name of the Lord?

*"By Your Name"*

# display |

You wouldn't speak poorly of your best friend, right? Because you love her and honor your relationship with her by respecting her, even when she's not around. Your relationship with Jesus is closer than anyone else in your life. Isn't He deserving of so much more respect? If you struggle with using His name in vain, try catching yourself and keeping track on your phone. At the end of the day, for each time you misused His name, think of a reason why His name is deserving of more respect. Ask for forgiveness, erase the list, and start fresh the next day. If you do not struggle using his name in vain, take some time to pray for those who do. Ask that God would help your vocabulary rub off on them.

Jesus, sometimes it's easy to misuse Your name. When it's not a big deal to the people I spend time with, it can be difficult for it to feel like a big deal to me. Forgive me for all of the times I have spoken Your name with emptiness. You are worthy of so much more than that.

# Praying With Open Hands

## discover |

READ MATTHEW 6:10A.

*"Your kingdom come. Your will be done."*

Do you think Jesus wanted to die on the cross? Do you think the perfect One who had never sinned would want to bear the weight of every sin past, present, and future? Matthew 26:39 says that the answer is no. When Jesus was in the garden of Gethsemane before being crucified, Scripture says, "he fell facedown and prayed, 'My Father, if it is possible, let this cup pass from me.'" Now, He could have stopped there, God could have granted His request, and life as a believer would look much different. (Picture a lot less quiet times and a lot more animal sacrifices.) Instead, He knew that there was a prophecy that needed to be fulfilled. A work that had begun that needed to be completed. He knew there was a girl reading this devotional who He loves and needed to give His life for. Instead of stopping there, He continued, "Yet not as I will, but as you will."

Jesus was the ultimate example for you. He sacrificed His own will for that of the Father because He knew there were greater things to accomplish for the kingdom that far outweighed His desire not to go to the cross. "Your kingdom come. Your will be done," means being okay with releasing your desires for your own kingdom for the will of God's kingdom. His will is perfect, so you can trust that it's worth it.

*"By Your Name"*

# delight |

**What is something you know the Lord has asked you to give up that you're holding on to?**

**If you were to make that sacrifice, what might you gain as a result?**

# display |

Releasing your desires for the sake of the kingdom looks different for everyone. It could mean sacrificing the exclusivity of your friend group to include a girl who you know needs a friend. It could mean sacrificing the plan you've made for your life because you know the Lord is calling you in a different direction. It could mean ending a relationship because that guy is holding you back from a deeper relationship with the Lord. Pray today with open hands, asking the Lord what you need to surrender to Him in order to live according to His will for your life.

Lord, let my heart's desire be to see Your kingdom come above all else. Your will for my life is to do what brings You glory, and if there's anything in my life that doesn't do that, please show me. I surrender every desire to You because I trust that Your will is best.

# As It Is in Heaven

## discover |

### READ MATTHEW 6:10B.

*". . .on earth as it is in heaven."*

"On earth as it is in heaven." You've heard it before, and it sounds cool, but what does it mean, really? Let's unpack it!

What is it about heaven? Heaven is the place for ultimate restoration. When God created people, He had an incredible plan for us; one that involved walking closely with Him from the moment we breathed our first breath. But then sin entered the world and pretty much ruined everything. Heaven is a place void of sin, void of separation from God, and full of eternal closeness and worship of the Father. It's the fulfillment of His original plan.

Why does God want earth to be like heaven? The only means of restoration we have on this side of eternity is a relationship with Jesus. It is His deepest desire for every living person to not only know Him but also to live for Him. That's the closest we'll get to heaven on earth.

What does that have to do with me? It starts with you! By praying "on earth as it is in heaven" every day, in every moment, you follow the example Jesus set for you—asking God to help you surrender your will for His. It starts with you so that it can happen through you.

# delight |

**What does today's culture communicate about surrendering control?**

**How is that message from society different from what the Lord says about surrendering control?**

**What is the outcome of listening to society versus following the Lord? (Hint: Read 1 John 2:17.)**

*"By Your Name"*

# display |

God doesn't need you. It sounds harsh, I know, but it's true! He is more than capable of accomplishing His will in His own power. And yet, He invites you to participate in bringing His kingdom to earth. He welcomes every prayer and every faith-driven effort with rejoicing.

1. Make it a part of your daily prayer time to ask the Lord how you can join Him in bringing heaven to earth each day.

2. Think of some girls you can invite to join you in this. There's power in praying together too!

Lord, I confess that surrendering control is difficult. It's easy to believe that only I know what's best for me because culture says giving up control means giving up power. So even when I don't understand it, help me trust Your will; I know that it's what's best.

# Nothing Is Too Small

## discover |

READ MATTHEW 6:11.

*"Give us today our daily bread."*

Imagine you didn't wake up in time for breakfast one day, and then at lunchtime, you realize you rushed out the door without grabbing your lunch. Both of your parents are at work and you don't have any money to buy lunch from the cafeteria. You go to your best friend and tell her you don't have any lunch. She turns back to you and says, "So? What do you want me to do about it?"

Can you imagine? More than likely, your best friend would never respond to you that way. I'm sure she would either share her lunch with you or help you figure out a way to get lunch for yourself. Best friends care about us too much to just leave us in need. Now imagine how much Jesus, who is closer to you than any friend or family member, cares about your needs. Knowing He cares gives you the freedom to ask for what you need. He wouldn't have made it a part of His model prayer if He didn't want you to ask!

"Daily bread" is the amount of bread needed to make it through the day. The Lord wants you to live in such a state of dependence on Him and His provision that you return to Him daily. He can and will supply all your needs—emotional, physical, and spiritual—according to His riches in glory (see Phil. 4:19). And those riches will never run out.

# delight |

**Why can it feel like God may not care about the small things in your life? How do you know He does care?**

**Read Matthew 6:25-34. How does knowing that God already knows what you need—both big and small things—change the way you pray?**

# display |

God cares about everyday things—from food and shelter to a disagreement with your parents to whether you pass a test—and He wants you to pray about them. Involve Him in the rhythm of your day-to-day life, asking for what you need as you experience those needs. There's nothing too small to ask for and nothing too big for Him to handle. In the space below, write out a request you consider small and a request you consider big. Pray about them both and trust God with how He answers.

Lord, it's amazing that You care about every single thing I care about. Please remind me as I move throughout my day to ask You for the things I need. Your Word says that You care for the birds and the wildflowers, and You love me way more than that, so I can trust that You will take care of me.

MEMORY VERSE
*Matthew 6:9-13*

"THEREFORE, YOU SHOULD
PRAY LIKE THIS:
OUR FATHER IN HEAVEN,
YOUR NAME BE HONORED
AS HOLY.
YOUR KINGDOM COME.
YOUR WILL BE DONE
ON EARTH AS IT IS IN HEAVEN.
GIVE US TODAY OUR
DAILY BREAD.
AND FORGIVE US OUR DEBTS,
AS WE ALSO HAVE FORGIVEN
OUR DEBTORS.
AND DO NOT BRING US
INTO TEMPTATION,
BUT DELIVER US FROM THE
EVIL ONE."

# Paid For

## discover |

*"And forgive us our debts. . ."*

No, you don't owe Jesus any money. This kind of debt forgiveness is not like the kind I wish the government had for my student loans. The debt being referenced is not monetary; it's a righteous debt, otherwise known as sin. God created you to live for His glory, but with sin in the picture, failure is unavoidable. Romans 3:23 is a reminder that everyone sins and falls short of the glory that God created us to pursue and reflect. With each sin, more debt accumulates, and the punishment should be death (see Rom. 6:23). But in His infinite mercy, Jesus became the payment for your sin when He died on the cross.

This part of the Lord's Prayer calls you to continually confess your sin and ask for forgiveness. It does you no good to deny your sinfulness. All denial does is create space between you and the Lord. 1 John 1:9 says, "If we confess our sins, he is faithful and righteous to forgive us our sins and to cleanse us from all unrighteousness." The moment you confess and ask for forgiveness, the slate is wiped clean. That's why daily prayer for forgiveness is so important: Jesus wants to forgive you! He always wants to be as close to you as possible at all times and doesn't want anything to stand in the way of that—especially unconfessed sin.

*Lifeway Girls | Devotions*   62

# delight |

**Has there been a time when sin made you feel far from God? Explain.**

**How did your relationship with God change after you confessed your sin to Him?**

# display |

Different sins have different consequences, but no sin is worse than another. For that reason, all sins need forgiveness. No sin is too small to confess. Take a moment right now to ask the Lord to bring to mind any sin that may be standing in the way of a closer relationship with Him. Confess your sin and ask for forgiveness.

Name a few girls around you who can pray for you and with you about any areas where you may be struggling with a certain sin. Having the support of others who are following Jesus too can create a safe space to share and be encouraged in your faith—even the tough parts!

Lord, I praise You for being such a gracious God and giving the gift of forgiveness so that nothing has to stand in between us. Help me to hate my sin as much as You do. Even in the moments I choose sin, remind me of Your grace so that I don't move away from You in shame but toward You in humility.

# Easier Said than Done

## discover |

READ MATTHEW 6:12B.

*". . .as we also have forgiven our debtors."*

Think of a girl who has wronged you. A name came into your mind pretty quickly, didn't it? That girl is your debtor, someone who has sinned against you. Maybe she said something hurtful to you or said something hurtful about you to someone else. Maybe she physically hurt you. Maybe she didn't do something to you directly, but her sin affected you. Whomever she is, whatever she did, you are called to forgive her. And according to the Lord's Prayer, you are called to forgive her of her sins before asking God to forgive you of yours. The prayer says, "And forgive us our debts, as we also have forgiven our debtors." That, my friend, is what they call past tense. Meaning, if you desire God's forgiveness, you must be willing to first forgive others. Sin in any capacity puts distance between you and the Father. Unconfessed sin, including unforgiveness, will hinder your relationship with Him.

It is vital to acknowledge that some forgiveness takes time. And that's okay. Your pain is justified, and God sees you and understands. All He asks of you is to confess it to Him. Confession is simply agreeing with God about your sin. Talk to Him about how badly you've been hurt, confess to Him that you're having trouble forgiving, and ask Him to help you. Because He is a gracious God who doesn't want anything to stand in the way of a close relationship with you, He will help.

# delight |

How are we called to forgive others? (Hint: Read Eph. 4:32.)

Why does it feel difficult to forgive others sometimes?

You are called to forgive even if you never receive an apology or even if the other person hasn't changed. How is that like the way God forgave you? (Hint: Read Rom. 5:8.)

# display |

Forgiveness is not weakness, and it is not reconciliation either. Reconciliation requires the other person to change; forgiveness does not. Forgiveness is God removing anger and resentment from your heart. The only way you can forgive is with His help. Think of the same girl who came to mind at the start of today's study. Confess to God that you're having trouble forgiving her, and ask Him to help you. You may need to seek external help as well, like therapy or counseling—both great tools the Lord has provided to help us heal. God will hear you and help you.

Lord, I confess that there is unforgiveness in my heart, and I've been hurt so deeply that it feels too big to get rid of. I don't want there to be anything between us, so I need Your help to forgive. Forgiving like You forgave me sounds easier said than done at this point. Thank You for the grace to take my time as I learn to forgive.

*"By Your Name"*

# Stay Ready

## discover |

### READ MATTHEW 6:13A.

*"And do not bring us into temptation. . .*

Temptation does not equal sin. That feels important to start with today because of how often it's not fully understood. In Matthew 4:1-11, Jesus was tempted by Satan in the desert and yet remained blameless and sinless. He wouldn't have been able to die on the cross as the perfect sacrifice if temptation was a sin. Even so, depending on how you handle it, temptation can lead to sin.

This portion of the Lord's Prayer is not meant to communicate that God is the One who leads you into temptation in the first place; He doesn't do that (see James 1:13-15). It is meant to encourage you to ask God to tune your heart to be aware of temptation and to flee from it. You wouldn't start training the morning of a marathon, and you wouldn't try to memorize a whole script right before opening night. God wants you to pray daily for protection from temptation so that when it comes, you will be prepared to fight it.

First Corinthians 10:13 makes it clear that you will face temptation, but you will not be fighting it alone. God, in His supreme faithfulness, "will also provide the way out so that you may be able to bear it." You have already been given victory over temptation in Christ Jesus. It's up to you to protect yourself against temptation so you can claim victory over it.

# delight |

**What is a temptation that is hard for you to resist?**

**How do you think your ability to fight that temptation would change if you prayed about it everyday?**

# display |

Temptation is inevitable, but it doesn't always have to mean defeat; it all depends on how you deal with it. Giving in to temptation gives way to guilt and shame. On the other hand, resisting temptation can lead to faith and wisdom: faith that God will help you overpower the temptation and wisdom regarding when you are most vulnerable to it and how to protect yourself.

Start praying over your weaknesses today so that temptation doesn't turn into sin. You have a choice: will you allow temptation to defeat you or refine you?

Though prayer should always be our first step when tempted, other believers can also help us. Think back to the girls you named on day 17 who could hold you accountable when you struggle. Consider which of those girls you could text or talk to when you're tempted so she can pray for and encourage you in that moment.

Lord, thank You for bringing to mind the temptations that I struggle with. There are times when I can't seem to win, and that is so discouraging. Please help defeat draw me closer to You instead of letting shame push me further away. I confess that I need Your help, and I trust that You will provide a way out every time I ask.

# Your Only Hope

## discover |

READ MATTHEW 6:13B.

*". . .but deliver us from the evil one."*

Do you remember the serpent in the garden of Eden? The one who tempted Eve, ruined God's perfect plan, and caused the rest of humanity to suffer in perpetuity as the consequence of sin? (See Gen. 3 for a refresher.) That serpent was none other than Satan—also known as the evil one—and he is powerful. Second Corinthians 11:14 says he "disguises himself as an angel of light." He makes himself out to be charming and enticing only to lure you away from the Lord and into sin. He knows if he can trap you in sin, you won't be doing anything for the kingdom.

Fear not, there is good news! You know Jesus, right? The One who conquered Satan and sin when He died on the cross? He rendered all of the enemy's schemes and lies powerless. If you have a relationship with the Lord, the same power that raised Christ from the dead lives in you by way of the Holy Spirit.

You shouldn't underestimate the power of the enemy, but you also can't forget about the power of the Savior. You have access to that power; all you have to do is ask. By praying for God to deliver you from the evil one, you are asking Him to rescue you from the traps set by the enemy—traps that would keep you bound to sin and away from the Lord. Prayer isn't your last resort against the evil one—it's your source of hope.

# delight |

**Why can it be difficult to recognize a trap of the enemy?**

**How does knowing you have the same power in you that raised Christ from the dead help you fight the evil one?**

# display |

The enemy can't control you or read your mind, but he does know your weak spots—sometimes better than you do. He knows which frustrating girl friend to use to get you to gossip, which apps most distract you from spending time with the Lord, and which temptation leads you to sin more often than not. He is clever, crafty, and yes, powerful. But take a moment to read Luke 10:19. Using an index card or creating a lock-screen for your phone, write out the words: *God's power can render the evil one powerless*. Get as creative as you like. Every time you see this phrase, let it remind you of the power God has given you over the enemy.

Lord, thank You for giving me Your power to fight against the evil one. You are my only hope of victory. Reveal to me all of my weak spots that the enemy could use to trap me in sin. I know You will strengthen each weak spot as I pray about them every day.

# What Jesus Prayed For

Jesus prayed for those around Him, He prayed for Himself, and He even prayed for you. This section highlights how having a relationship with the Father doesn't just mean you can talk to Him about anything, it also means He wants you to.

# Sifted

## discover |

READ LUKE 22:31-34.

*"Simon, Simon, look out. Satan has asked to sift you like wheat. But I have prayed for you that your faith may not fail. And you, when you have turned back, strengthen your brothers."*
*—Luke 22:31-32*

I'm willing to bet you don't already know what it means to sift wheat. But don't feel bad—I didn't either. It's the process of separating the wheat (the good stuff) from the chaff (the useless stuff). The wheat is put into a large strainer—perhaps one with jagged edges—and violently shaken until anything clinging to the grain is shaken off and filtered out. Basically, sifting wheat was meant to break it apart and break it down. That's exactly what Satan said he wanted to do to Simon (aka Peter) and the disciples: break them down.

The "you" in this passage is plural; Jesus was talking to all of the disciples. He was letting them know Satan had a plan to destroy their faith. Satan wanted to sift them through trial and hardship so they would come out the other side faithless. He operates the same way today. The enemy wants to rid you of your faith, whether by suffering (the book of Job) or prosperity (Judas; see Matt. 26:14-16), so that you will stop living for the Lord. But don't be discouraged! Remember that Jesus prays for you, or intercedes, in the same way He did for the disciples. Satan may be powerful, but his power is extinguished by Christ's intercession. The Lord's desire is not to see you destroyed but to see you refined so that, like Simon and the disciples, when you emerge from a trial, your story to tell is one of victory and steadfast faith.

# delight |

**How does it feel to know that the Lord Himself prays on your behalf?**

**Describe a circumstance where you've felt like sifted wheat: broken down without much faith. How did you see God bring you through that season?**

*"By Your Name"*

# display |

There is a reason the Lord allows difficult things to happen to you. He does not delight in seeing you struggle. The Lord wants the same thing for you as He did for the disciples: sanctification, or to be made to look more like Him (James 1:2-4). He prays for you to come out on the other side of the trial full of faith and ready to strengthen the faith of others through your story.

If you are going through a trial right now, take a moment and focus on the reality that Jesus is praying for you. Ask Him for strength to endure it and come out on the other side with a deeper faith.

Write out the names of some girls you know who are also going through some tough stuff. Spend a minute praying for those girls' faith to be strengthened and thanking Jesus that He's praying for them too.

Thank You, Lord, for all of the times You kept the enemy from sifting me like wheat. Help me also be thankful for all the times You didn't. I'll admit that there have been some really hard times when I just don't see the good yet. But I trust You, and that means I can trust that goodness is on its way.

# Do As I Say and As I Do

discover |

READ JOHN 12:27-36.

*"Now my soul is troubled. What should I say—Father, save me from this*
*hour? But that is why I came to this hour. Father, glorify your name."*
*Then a voice came from heaven: "I have glorified it, and I will glorify it again."*
*—John 12:27-28*

It would have been very easy for Jesus to say, "Your will be done" to the Father for all of the "good" parts of His ministry—performing miracles, teaching crowds of people, traveling with twelve of His closest friends. The real test came when it was time to face the worst thing that would happen to Him: enduring the cross. So what did Jesus do when it was time to face it? He prayed. (It's almost like He wants you to understand something about prayer.)

Jesus has never led by a "do as I say, not as I do" example; everything He instructs you to do, He practiced Himself. Even in the passage you just read, He abided by the same structure of prayer that He outlined in the Lord's Prayer. In His most difficult moment, He acknowledged God's name as holy and asked for His will to be done.

It is relatively painless to trust God when things are going well in your life. Praying "Your will be done" doesn't feel like a gamble when you think His will for you is just going to be more goodness. Jesus knew what was going to happen to Him and still prayed the same way. He surrendered to the will of the Father even though it meant suffering for Himself. The instruction to ask that God's will be done in and through you extends to the difficult times as well.

# delight |

**Name two other things in Scripture Jesus asks you to do that He was willing to do Himself.**

**How does knowing Jesus followed the example He set for you help you obey Him?**

# display |

Giving up your own desires is not an easy thing to do. Giving up your desires when they may be replaced with suffering is an even harder thing to do. The longer you know the Lord, the more inevitable it's going to be that you struggle. But just like Jesus, you can pray for yourself and ask the Lord for strength to not only get through it but also come out on the other side rejoicing. In the space below, write out, "Your will be done." Make these words as pretty and creative as you like. Then, dwell on those words and pray them over the situations you are facing in your life. If it's tough, tell Him. He can and wants to help you through it.

Lord, I know there is no easy way around tough times. The only way I'll get through them is with You. Even if it's not what I would have chosen for my life, I pray that Your will be done. I'm confident that even though it may not be what I want, Your will is always what I need.

# What's in Your Heart?

## discover |

### READ JOHN 17:1-2.

*Jesus spoke these things, looked up to heaven, and said, "Father, the hour has come. Glorify your Son so that the Son may glorify you, since you gave him authority over all people, so that he may give eternal life to everyone you have given him."*

Our most genuine self is revealed in prayer. Our deepest feelings, hurts, and motivations easily come to the surface when talking to the Lord. Luke 6:45 says, "for his mouth speaks from the overflow of the heart." Today's Scripture gives a unique insight into the heart of Jesus. His public prayer made it clear that the contents of His heart were formed in the moments of private prayer with the Father.

Scripture makes it evident that Jesus did not want to bear the cross. Could He have accomplished the will of the Father by any other means, I'm sure He would have done it. When pressure was applied to His life, and He prepared to take on the worst thing to be set before Him, the overflow of His heart was fear and despair. Wait a second; that's not true! The overflow of His heart was unwavering faith that His death and resurrection were purposeful in bringing about the will of the Father. To the world, and certainly to the people of Jesus's time, the cross may be a symbol of humiliation. But to Jesus, it was an instrument of glorification and the means by which He gets to offer you everlasting life.

# delight |

**What does the way you speak say about the contents of your heart?**

**Do you think the way you live shows people that you spend time with the Lord? Why or why not?**

# display |

Stress tends to bring out the worst in people. They're more irritable, moody, and pessimistic. When Jesus was (to put it lightly) under stress, out of Him flowed peace and confidence. He had spent time with His Father and was focused on bringing Him glory.

When pressure is applied in your life, what's spilling out of you? Fear and doubt or peace and confidence? Take a minute to journal your thoughts.

Start your time in prayer today by praying Psalm 139:23-24. You've done it before, but this time, ask the Lord to reveal to you the true contents of your heart and get rid of anything that is not glorifying to Him.

> Lord, it is my sole purpose as a believer to bring You glory, and it's my desire that everything about my life would do that. Bring to mind the things I may be holding onto that could hold me back from bringing You glory: selfishness, pride, anger, unforgiveness, or even apathy. I surrender those things and ask You to fill my heart with only the best things: faith, hope, and love.

# Only One Way

discover |

READ JOHN 17:3-5.

*This is eternal life: that they may know you, the only true God, and the
one you have sent —Jesus Christ. I have glorified you on the earth by
completing the work you gave me to do. Now, Father, glorify me in your
presence with that glory I had with you before the world existed.*

The world thinks there are several ways to eternal life—other religions,
working to earn it, or being "good enough." In this prayer to the Father,
Jesus was clear that the only way to eternal life is through Him. The
same thing is true now as it was then: Jesus has no greater desire than
for everyone to be in relationship with Him. That was the reason He
came to earth. That was the reason He fulfilled the will of God and died
on the cross, even though He didn't want to (see day 14). His death
on the cross is what allows you to be in relationship with Him, and
relationship with Him is what gives you eternal life.

The gift of eternal life is an unpopular concept in today's world. We
have been trained to believe every good thing should be earned. You
earn money by working. You earn approval by being the best or the
nicest. You earn rest through accomplishment. Our brains are hardwired
to believe that if it's not something we earned, it must come with
strings attached. Eternal life is the most no-strings-attached gift you will
ever be offered. With His prayers, Jesus wanted everyone to know the
truth: eternal life is free, but it's only through Him. If you want to care
for others in the same way Jesus did, your life and your prayers should
aim to communicate the same truth.

# delight |

**What are some ways you've heard people say they can gain eternal life?**

**What is your role in helping people understand the way to eternal life?**

# display |

The fact that eternal life is a gift is truly a blessing. The Lord knew that if it was something to be earned, humans would never rest from trying to achieve it. That is why so many people get burnt out on religion and performance—they're trying everything to earn something that can only be attained through salvation and a relationship with Jesus.

Consider the girls closest to you. Do they know the source of eternal life? Spend five minutes today praying for the girls who don't, and ask the Lord to show you your part in leading them toward salvation.

Lord, I believe eternal life can only be found through You. I want to share Your heart for the people who don't know You. Let it be my deepest desire to see those I love come to know You. Help me to talk about it often and with urgency.

*"By Your Name"*

John 17:20-21

I PRAY NOT ONLY FOR
THESE, BUT ALSO FOR
THOSE WHO BELIEVE
IN ME THROUGH THEIR
WORD. MAY THEY ALL BE
ONE, AS YOU, FATHER, ARE
IN ME AND I AM IN YOU.
MAY THEY ALSO BE IN US,
SO THAT THE WORLD MAY
BELIEVE YOU SENT ME.

# Bubble Burst

## discover |

READ JOHN 17:6-19.

*"I am not praying that you take them out of the world but*
*that you protect them from the evil one."*
*—John 17:15*

The disciples were on a mission. They had been tasked with carrying the gospel during Jesus's earthly ministry and, more importantly, after. Jesus had equipped them for ministry so that when He finally ascended into heaven, the Lord's work on earth didn't leave with Him (see Acts 1:8-9). When Jesus prayed for the disciples, He was clear that He did not want them taken out of the world. To clarify, that was not His way of asking God not to kill them. He was confirming with God that He wouldn't shelter them so much that they would turn inward into a "Christian bubble"—a place where they had to risk nothing for the sake of the gospel like time, comfort, or safety. The disciples' mission required them to be in the world; that much was unavoidable. Jesus prayed for the disciples' protection so they could continue spreading word of the Lord without interference from the evil one.

Your mission on this earth is the same as the disciples', and God's desire for you is the same as it was for them. He has called you not to be physically set apart from the world in your Christian bubble but to be spiritually set apart, or holy. As you fulfill your mission of sharing the gospel, God will protect you from the evil one.

# delight |

At what times do you find yourself being of the world and not just in the world?

Why do you think you need more protection from the enemy when you're following the Lord closely?

# display |

When you follow the Lord closely, everything you do changes. The way you
live your life draws people to want to know the One who changed you. That is
wholly pleasing to the Lord, but it is the last thing the enemy wants. He wants to
do everything in His power to defeat you and halt the movement of the gospel
one person at a time. Don't let him! Be vigilant in praying for protection from
the evil one daily. Ask the Lord to protect you in the same way He protected the
disciples so they could accomplish their mission. Then pray the same thing for
the girls around you who are also following Jesus closely.

Lord, growing in my relationship with You just puts a target on my
back from the enemy. He will do whatever it takes to keep me from
living for You. I know You are more powerful than any attack from
the enemy, and I trust You will protect me as I continue getting closer
to You.

# The Time-Traveling Prayer

## discover |

### READ JOHN 17:20-26.

*"I pray not only for these, but also for those who believe in me through their word. May they all be one, as you, Father, are in me and I am in you. May they also be in us, so that the world may believe you sent me."*
—*John 17:20-21*

Would you believe me if I told you that on the night of His crucifixion, Jesus prayed for you? Because He did! And He prayed for me too. Jesus didn't pray for us each by name (at least in as much as Scripture documents), but He did pray for all believers—the church, the body of believers—that would be for the rest of time. His request to the Father was for our unity, that our oneness would rightly represent Jesus to the world.

For most people, "unified" is not the first word that comes to mind when thinking about the contemporary church. There has been disagreement and division over things like denominations, politics, and personal convictions. Grave moral failures by well-known believers and unsteady stances on injustices have made the church seem fickle to those on the outside looking in. Jesus knew this is what it would be like. In His infinite wisdom, on the night of His crucifixion, He prayed for us who are a part of the present-day church. Whether we live like it or not, that prayer was answered. Consider this: when you disagree with your family, they don't cease to be your family. Likewise, the church is not any less the body of Christ in discord than it is in harmony. It is up to believers to trust that Jesus's prayer for unity was answered so that wherever there is a lack of unity, there follows a desire for restoration.

# delight |

Do you think the present-day church looks the way God originally intended?

What is the church missing out on when it operates in disunity?

What part can you play in the unification of the church? (Hint: Read 2 Cor. 13:11.)

# display |

Jesus desires unity in the church as a reflection of His unity with the Father. It can be challenging to know where to start when tackling such a complex issue. When it feels overwhelming to think about, remember it starts with you. You can't control the beliefs or actions of any other believer besides yourself.

Humbly ask the Lord where you could be doing more to unify the church. Unity is worth pursuing because community with others is worth pursuing. Everyone is on the same ground at the foot of the cross.

Think of a few girls you struggle to be unified with. Ask God to reveal to you how to pursue greater unity with them. Then, take whatever steps He leads you to take.

Lord, thank You for seeing beyond the present to pray for believers in the future. Give me Your heart to see unity in the church. I confess that sometimes it feels easier just to remain indifferent and not even try to change anything, but I know that's not how You want me to live. Remind me that Your prayer for the church's unity was answered, and help me be a part of the restoration.

*"By Your Name"*

# The Giver of Good Gifts

## discover |

READ MARK 14:32-42.

*And he said, "Abba, Father! All things are possible for you. Take this cup*
*away from me. Nevertheless, not what I will, but what you will."*
*—Mark 14:36*

You can ask God for whatever you want: new friends, for your crush to return your affections, a good grade on an exam. Literally anything. Jesus revealed in His prayer for Himself in the garden of Gethsemane that it is okay to pray for yourself and for a specific outcome. Jesus was so deeply distressed by the cross—not because of the physical pain that awaited Him but because of the spiritual torment. In 2 Corinthians 5:21, it says, "He made the one who did not know sin to be sin for us." Jesus was perfect and, before the cross, He never knew sin. He knew the cup set before Him meant becoming sin, and that grieved Him to His core. It makes complete sense that He would ask God to take the cup from Him. Even so, when He cried out to God to spare Him, Jesus was intentional to not omit consideration for the greater plan of the Father. In His hour of greatest need and profound want, His posture was still one of humility, surrendering His desires to the will of the Father "so that in him we might become the righteousness of God" (2 Cor. 5:21).

The more time you spend with God, the more your desires will align with His. As you grow in your relationship with God, you'll be able to ask Him for whatever you want because it will be what He wants too.

# delight |

**Do you consider what the Lord may want for you when you pray? Why or why not?**

**How do you get your desires to align with the Lord's desires for you?**

# display |

Is there something you've been holding onto, too afraid to ask Jesus for it? Maybe you have a big dream you're too scared to even talk about—reconciliation in your parents' relationship you're scared to hope for or a hurt so deep that you don't know if it could be healed even if you asked. Think of what you've been holding. Ask God for it, and be specific! Ask with open hands as a representation that you are surrendering your will and you're open to receive from Him, the Giver of good gifts (see James 1:17). Remember, Jesus didn't get what He asked for, but He asked for it regardless. Ask the Lord in faith and trust His response.

Lord, thank You for every good thing I have; I know I wouldn't have anything apart from You. You have proven Yourself to be the giver of good gifts. May that move me to ask boldly for the things I want and accept graciously whatever it is You have for me.

# He Can Handle It

## discover |

READ MATTHEW 27:45-46.

*From noon until three in the afternoon, darkness came over the whole land. About three in the afternoon Jesus cried out with a loud voice, "Elí, Elí, lemá sabachtháni?" that is, "My God, my God, why have you abandoned me?"*

During His earthly ministry, Jesus was fueled by His relationship with God. He was constantly talking to Him, teaching about Him, and doing everything for His glory. That is why this moment on the cross was worse than any other moment in His life. He had endured physical pain and even emotional pain, but He had never known silence from His Father. The very second Jesus became sin for us (see 2 Cor. 5:21), Jesus experienced the weight of all the sins of the world and the fullness of God's wrath at the same time.

When Jesus cried out to God to ask why He had abandoned Him, He was quoting Psalm 22. Psalm 22 is considered a Messianic psalm, meaning it would be connected to the one the Jews thought would come to save them. Jesus quoted this psalm to let those witnessing His death know one last time that He is the Messiah. He was also asking a genuine and difficult question of His Father.

The Lord can handle your difficult questions too. When you feel angry at God, sad about life, or forsaken and alone and you don't understand why, take your questions to God. He won't be caught off guard—He already knows, and He can handle it.

# delight |

**Have you ever felt abandoned by God? What is His promise to you? (Hint: Read Deut. 31:6.)**

**What is a difficult question you've asked God? How did He answer?**

# display |

God promises to never leave or forsake you. That means you can trust that He's always going to be available for you to talk to about your biggest questions and deepest feelings. God can handle your emotions—He created them. Having questions or even doubts doesn't make you a "bad" Christian. All the Lord asks is that you pray. Instead of ignoring your emotions, go to Him with your questions and doubts and ask for clarity. You may not ever have a clear answer for everything on this side of eternity, but it never hurts to ask. If there is a big question you have for God, write it below. In faith, ask Him and see what He says. Be patient. Sometimes it's in waiting for the answer that we learn the lesson He is teaching us through the circumstance.

> **Lord, thank You for Your promise to never leave me. It gives me peace to know that no matter what I do or say, You're not going anywhere. Let that knowledge motivate me to ask You tough questions. Grant me understanding, and help me have faith even without fully understanding. Even without all of the answers, I still trust You.**

*"By Your Name"*

# You Can Trust Him

## discover |

READ LUKE 23:46.

*And Jesus called out with a loud voice, "Father, into your hands I entrust my spirit." Saying this, he breathed his last.*

Jesus was only on the cross for about six hours. In general, that is a long time to be endlessly tortured. However, other victims of crucifixion sometimes suffered for two or three days before death befell them. That just proves Jesus gave up His life only when He wanted to and only when the work He was put on the cross to do was finished. His final prayer on the cross was a declaration of His trust in God—trust that His plan was good and His will is always best.

When you have confidence that the Lord's way is best, you can put your full trust in Jesus. The chances of Him asking you to sacrifice your life on a cross are next to none. He may, however, ask you to sacrifice other things—friendships, jobs, time—to fulfill His purpose in your life. You can sacrifice joyfully, knowing your life isn't in the hands of some malevolent ruler who just wants to use you as He sees fit with no regard for your well-being. He is such a good Father that He wants His will to be done while also truly desiring the best for you. Trusting Him may look a little mysterious at times, but it is always worth it.

# delight |

**When have you been hesitant to trust God with something? Why?**

**How does understanding Jesus trusted the Father with His life help you to trust Him with yours?**

# display |

As a kid, you were taught to stay away from strangers because you don't know them. That's why you have to put in the time and effort to know the Lord. If you don't know the nature of His heart and how He feels about you as His child, there's no way you can fully trust Him. Read Romans 8:28. Take time to reflect on knowing everything works out "for the good of those who love Him, who are called according to His purpose." How does this help you fully trust the Lord?

Lord, I pray that as my knowledge of You grows, so will my trust in You. You have proven to be a Man of Your Word not only in Scripture but also over and over again in my own life. Help me to trust You with my whole heart no matter the circumstance because I know everything will work together for good.

# Still Emmanuel

## discover |

### READ LUKE 24:13-25.

*It was as he reclined at the table with them that he took the bread, blessed and broke it, and gave it to them. Then their eyes were opened, and they recognized him, but he disappeared from their sight.*
*—Luke 24:30-31*

Three days after Jesus's crucifixion, two disciples were walking on a seven-mile journey to a nearby town called Emmaus. They were discussing and arguing about the events of the past few days. As they were walking, Jesus appeared and started walking with them. He spoke with them about their questions surrounding His crucifixion. Still, they did not know it was Jesus. They explained to Him the story of His own death and the prophecy surrounding it. Still, they did not know it was Jesus. After arriving at their destination, they sat down for a meal, and Jesus took the bread, blessed it, and broke it. It wasn't until then that their eyes were opened and they knew it was Jesus.

Prayer isn't just a personal suggestion box for you to make requests for all the good things you want for your life. Prayer is a two-sided conversation that, yes, does include requests, but it is also how you get to know who Jesus is. If you let it, life will distract you from knowing the Lord. There will always be something—school, relationships, social media, TV—that will keep you from really seeing Jesus if you don't make Him a priority. He could be moving and doing incredible things all around you, but like the disciples on the road, you could miss seeing Him. If you stay in consistent communication with God, you will know Him. And when you know Him, you will recognize His work in you and around you.

# delight |

What distractions have kept you from seeing Jesus?

If you knew Jesus would do one thing in your life if only you prayed for it, what would you want to see Him do?

# display |

Jesus is Emmanuel, "God with us." How sad to think that He could be walking with you and talking to you, but you're missing it because you're distracted. Take a moment to think about your answers to the question about what distracts you. Ask the Lord to reveal to you why you have valued those things more than time with Him. Ask yourself if those reasons are worth missing out on the work of the Lord. (Hint: They're not!) Nothing is impossible for Him to do. You just have to stay consistent in prayer, and He will do the rest.

Lord, I don't want to miss a single thing You're doing. I confess that I've allowed other things to distract me, but I want to reset. Thank You that I can reset every day and even every moment through prayer. Remind me to focus on You.

# Is There Another Way?

From His baptism, to the quiet moments when He went away alone to connect with the Father, to His crucifixion, Jesus showed us what it means to take all things to God in prayer. While we can't say Jesus was struggling to do what God asked, we do know He faced every kind of temptation we face (see Heb. 4:15). But Jesus perfectly modeled for us what to do when we have tough questions: go to God.

Let's look at two specific examples in Scripture.

Jesus asked one of the questions as He was praying in the garden of Gethsemane just before His trial and crucifixion. Jesus had just told His disciples that He was "deeply grieved to the point of death" (Matt. 26:38). Then,

> *Going a little farther, he fell facedown and prayed,*
> *"My Father, if it is possible, let this cup pass from me.*
> *Yet not as I will, but as you will."*
> *—Matthew 26:39*

It wasn't that Jesus was questioning God's plan—His posture is one of both humility and submission to God's authority—but Jesus knew the shame, the pain, and the abandonment that lay ahead. He knew His Father was good and had a plan that was ultimately good, but that didn't mean it would be easy and pain-free. In fact, it would be quite the opposite. Cue the second question:

> *"My God, my God, why have you abandoned me?"*
> *—Matthew 27:46*

Jesus took on God's wrath for our sin, and in that moment, God was silent. Even though Jesus had known this was God's plan from the beginning, we still see Him cry out in deep distress with this question. And in a way, our questions sometimes mirror His. Maybe we, too, sometimes want to know:

**God, is there another way?**

**God, why is _____ a reality? God, why is _____ happening? Or, simply: God, why?**

Asking a question doesn't have to amount to questioning God's goodness or plan. While we must be careful to keep a right perspective of who God is when we talk to Him; it's not a bad thing to ask Him a question. Like Jesus, may we use our toughest questions to direct our hearts toward the One who has every answer, saying with Jesus, "Not as I will, but as you will."

**Take a minute and ask the Holy Spirit to guide you as you examine your heart: what tough questions are you struggling with right now? Jot them down in the space provided. Then, just like Jesus modeled for us, spend some time asking God your tough questions.**

# How To Pray Like Jesus

On days 23–26, we looked at what's often called Jesus's Farewell Prayer or High Priestly prayer (see John 17). This prayer is the final part of His farewell discourse (chs. 13–17), where Jesus prepared His disciples for the time when He would no longer be with them. The prayer itself can be broken down into several sections that help us see, once again, how to pray like Jesus.

Read John 17 in your Bible and jot down notes about what Jesus prayed for each of these people or groups.

**1. Jesus prayed for Himself (see John 17:1-5).**

**2. Jesus prayed for His disciples (see John 17:6-19).**

**3. Jesus prayed for future believers (see John 17:20-26).**

While not everything will apply to you—especially in the section where Jesus prayed for Himself—jot down some ideas of how you can model your own prayer after Jesus's prayer. One example has been filled in for each section.

**I can pray for myself:**
**(Ex., That I will glorify God with my life.)**

**I can pray for other Christians today:**
**(Ex., That they will be filled with the joy of Christ.)**

**I can pray for future believers:**
**(Ex., That they will experience unity.)**

**Now, taking the list you just made, spend some time praying aloud or write out a prayer below.**

# Notes